G000059992

The Sound of Blossom Falling

A Collection of Poetry

by

Vincent Berquez

'Dedicated to my wife, Ali, and my son, Etienne.'

Contents

ME

A walk on Hilly Fields with my dog, Kenny

There was no need, no need to look
at the blood, the blood spattered
on my shirt and arms and hands.

Hands carrying, laden with a dog,
the dog with his neck gouged out.
Fur in lumps removed from his neck.

This neck was red, red with the blood
from the fight, the fight with the Red Setter
that had attacked and mauled my little dog.

My dog Kenny in my arms, in my bloody arms,
whimpering sadly, unable to lick his neck covered in pain,
looked in shock around him, unable to comprehend.

And the searing pain in my hand, carrying my dog,
covered in blood, with a hole in my palm from the attack,
red with blood, painfully red from the Red Setter.

In the park, the dog attacked viciously,
biting deeply into the neck of my dog. The owner tried valiantly
to restrain, to restrain the vicious thrashing of those pointed teeth.

And those sharp teeth crunched into flesh.
Me, an eleven-year-old panicking, watching his dog yowl
with pain, skin and fur torn off from his neck, powerless to stop it.

And the owner lashed out, whipping repeatedly
the savage beast with his lead, crying her eyes out,
as the dog bit in a frenzy at the fur of my animal.

And in slow motion, my memory
Recalls how I punched the dog attacking,
punched it in its mouth as hard as I could.

Without thought, I forced my fist into its mouth,
into its jaw, as it bit down on my hand with all its force,
teeth cutting into my flesh, injuring my small hand.
As I punched it in the mouth, the force shocked it,
shocked and startled it, until its eyes regained its brain
and ran away, mouth covered in our blood and flesh.

The shaking owner, sobbing, went running after
the punched dog, shouting hysterically, trying to catch it,
leaving me on the grass with my startled dog panting.

Lurching to my feet, I heaved him into my arms
and carried him from the park, walking to my home,
blood mingling as I struggled down the road terrified.

And then nothing, there was nothing left in me as I fainted
at the doorstep to regain some form of consciousness,
as my grandmother started to shout in French to rouse the household.

She picked me up, leaving Kenny on the step,
whining to himself, blood sticky on his fur, red raw flesh
oozing his pain, not able to move or understand.

I was led into the kitchen before I vomited and passed out again.

It would be months before we both recovered and healed
and went for another walk.

Being Voltaire out of age

I am so very late for now that the grainy ink fossil-dried amid
melted arteries of candle wax and with dusty dirt-snuff has
formed a mountain range of streaked melding sentences
bleeding like a Roman in his last act of heroic foolishness,
unformed words trickled down the dusted rutted source and away.

I have come too far from my time of penned curves and waves,
powdered and pampered amid the squalor and poverty of plagues
I recited puddles of salty tales and shiny flintlock balls of poetry
into the minds imprisoned in the time of mirrors in the age of death.

In that dry age we searched for a real oasis to sup ourselves dry,
drinking the blue liquid deeply as we searched for other meanings,
drinking the red liquid when the solutions seemed absurd, we vanished.

Words are mostly technical or medical, financial or psychological now,
a suggested time becoming more divorced from the cosmic as you do so
leaves the flames small but the man is impotent and ready
for his destruction.

The era of dream makers and devil takers has passed into
the deepest crevice,
into the mouth-moat far away and I am too late for the theme
of time to change.

Boarding School Blues

I was a small animal live and savage and knew all the ways to be clever.
I was a Hussar, a charger, a stallion and I was stronger.
When I was sent there, it was to aid my mother's escape:
to break her out of the cycle of living with my father.
I was sent to a place bucolic: not for an urbanite - not me – not city.
I thought buying uniforms and stuff exciting.
Trying on my school jacket I didn't realise the racket,
it was to imprison me in this strange place.
The first days I sobbed out loud – not too loud - covering my face
with a blanket, a shroud to hide my embarrassment of shame and pain.
I was a little lion, a boy child, a Kim. Thought not too big I began
to believe in my self-importance and preponderance.
So, I stopped crying and started to do some fighting:
beating and being beaten by larger and smaller animals than myself.
I didn't always fight fair. Sometimes I was Tarzan smashing up weaklings,
soft as marzipan in my grip. I could be a vicious pig.
I was bullied and got what I got, I got the lot, broken fingers,
cut lips, bruises and pains, black eyes and bloody noses, thrown
into bushes of stinging nettles and rose bushes.

There was no stopping me without the control of a parental animal.
I was missing my mother and father and grandmother and brother
and dog and cat and neighbourhood and sweet shop and television
and friends and the secret areas and camps and gardens, and all
the archetypes of the he-child, I missed the lot.
I learnt to run. I learnt to hide and got my hide tanned by some
perverted excuse for a schoolmaster.
I discovered my inner roar. I was taught to read and write all day

and slept with my bum to the wall at night from the nightly exploits.
I sang psalms in an off-key voice, looked at the masters and thought
they were cowards, losers and false heroes.
I would have bitten them apart, chewed them up and spat them out.

FATHER CHRISTMAS, YOU OLD FRAUD!

I found God in a sock when I was five years old.

He left me a bag of soldiers and a baffling wooden puzzle

when I was taken to visit him. He didn't scare me

when I sat on his knee in the plasticated grotto.

All the little wolverines waited behind me

hungry for crap toys they would break or that would seize-up.

He wore a polyester beard and felt clothes and smelt of No.6 cigarettes,

of discarded promises and unrealistic wishes. Afterwards I waited

all night for him by the chimney stack hoping he would burn his arse

on the glowing logs below, but no one came and, in the morning,

I got a Joe 90 kit and a toy bazooka that did everything for me.

Amen.

Inland

I am lustful for the sea to be within
for the shore to rasp my feet for the water
to cover its sheet about my body and cover
this city lightly and then darkly the shingle to tickle
my senses and secrets.

I am lustful for the sea to transport this man of slate
far away from the mountains of plastic and carouse
in exploding waves breaking the shouting of cars
and crying of polluted false winds.

I am lustful to be drenched
and to remove the smoke from before my eyes
to wash me to make me swim in currents
far from streets of hopeless discourses.

I am lustful to sink in the sands and not in me
to splash in a strong adhesive away from the glue
away from the quag-dosage of the city's condition.

And when the cyano-night comes at me
I am lustful for the sounds of glassy chattering
to come calling for the sea to be lusting for me.

Keeping up

My hand slipped out as he walked
faster than I could. He stood taller,
above me, a giant shadow glancing,
glowering from on high and carried on.

I saw his hand moving away. He marched
faster, pushing forward without mine.
He carried on regardless of my small feet,
of my size and age, his own aim was all.

I tripped over myself to keep up with him
as his big feet turned the road's corner.
I raced to make sure I didn't lose him,
I could hear the sound of his disapproval
as I tried to keep up or get his hand back.

My dog shot a face from the short wall
anxiously, as if he sensed my inner panic
in his flitting eyes and sniffy movements.
He glanced and skittled back to the big feet,
he was just letting me know I wasn't lost.

I knew these roads well; old trees had meaning.
I noticed familiar things that seemed odd to me,
the graffiti and grubbiness pervaded everything,
many messy secret sins behind strangers' doors
felt too close when I walked secretly past them.

My soggy woollen coat smelt of sweat as I ran
slowly, dragging my little body behind myself,
breathing heavy, full of my own complaints.
The corner came before me and I was there,
in front of the supermarket. My father disappeared
into its ugly plastic mouth with my dog closely by
and I kicked stones outside as a childish protest.

The great book of time

I read the great book of time in my sleep,
each leaf puffed out and blew away easily,
words flutterered in my face, a surface imagined,
grasped. The light grappled through the cerebral
like a cut out of reality, accessed and precocious.

The book just vibrated, a flash flickered
towards me, as letters flew from the confines
of the pages' tyranny.

The great book of time is constantly murdered,
killed and integrated, smothered in thoughts
of hatred and death.
Maybe something fragile appears – like my life.
It becomes a memory breathed
by others momentarily and vanishes in the stars.

Mother with dementia

1.
I must care for you, no longer the proud flower.
You must travel now towards your destiny's end.
Slowly, on your crippled stems, the colourful flower you were.
Each movement in agony by the dagger of osteoporosis
In your seed's anatomy. Your autonomy felled,
your personality destroyed. In the ground of earth,
your roots gripping hold desperately.

2.
I have to lift and listen to your dry leaves,
crisp and arid, disjointed, enfeebled.
You sag and heave your bony frame slowly,
taking moribund strides, life beating still.
One part in one camp, the next, towards the void.

3.
To be grounded and plucked, stuck awaiting life
To suck the last footstep, the last movement
That the brain disdains, what the body clearly restrains.

4.
The fruit salad of her mind, the spaghetti of her brain.
The liquorice all sorts of her psyche, the fruit and nut of her life.
A blancmange of demented mush slowly losing its grip on
the grip of life.

5.
Her hair unwashed and clothes soiled.
Bruised blushed skin cracked and withered.
Knuckles protruding through tight and loose skin.
Deadened eyes always talking pointlessly.
She is always telling me, as I try to reason to a shrinking shell
about the whys and wherefores, and of course, the confusion.

6.
The walking stick stability stalks the inability of life to reason
in the confusion, in the very grain of reality that the brain is saying
there is no longer a seed, but a husk, a dried-out grain is dying.

My Punk revolution

At 15 the revolution in my head was confusion.
The word 'belief' was one I didn't use at all
and in a supremely hyperactive gobby way,
I splashed the maelstrom and became anti-everything.

In the world, noise was being machine-gunned,
music argued for, hysterical requiems of the old
and impossible manic apogees for the young
were virulently discussed, which I didn't understand.

Explaining place, time and meaning is in truth impossible
as memory leaks and solidifies and unripe energy -
the god of change – youthful, unlearnt, powerful, screeches out
claiming originality and the rest becomes bones picked over.

It was another raw birthday and I wanted to
escape my life of stupid ignorance and experience
so with the money I was reluctantly given
I went out and bought too-expensive Punk clothes.

I can't remember now if I had ever travelled
the vast way to Chelsea alone before
so I became an explorer, an adventurer,
challenging my fears and ventured forth.

I self-consciously labelled myself, seared,
I began walking the streets, angry, red-faced
searching for a place that would take me in,
give me a voice to begin my independence.

Through my misty fog of trampling busy streets
I met more confusion than I had inherited:
the music was mostly inept, awful and so were
the furious musicians with their attitude and little else.

My mother, the soprano, appalled by my recent choices
said 'I told you so' in her put-on shrill intonation,
warbling hysterically to me why should I look further than the best
instead of rifling through musical dustbins for rubbish?

Drenched in alcohol my father said immature politics
were the same that created wars and pointless death
so why be a victim of social and political fashion,
as you should know better from your expensive education...

I didn't understand the revolutions of thought
in the heads of my annoying parents and sulked away,
chaffed from the tight plastic trousers, blistered
from crap footwear, ears ringing.from too loud music.

Proof Reader at the Financial Times

The grumbling mumbler with the pug nose
and taught rubbery banded lips
splats outwards the naggy nuisance
of his corroding explicatory jargon.
Fingering forward, the stabby path
of his disjointed pointer, stabbing at it
like a stapler on amphetamines.
Down the page his squinty eyes pass,
dripping the criticism outwards
with 1000 complex reasons why,
which has nothing to do with mistakes.

Here and here - the culprit - who is me,
sits there and is partly prodded
and poked at verbally and accused
of being a simple-minded moron
in a few of the juiciest and choicest words.

The page is pushed aside for the next
scuffling words, words that scalpel,
words that don't cheat the shudder
explode like a detonation ignited.

Grumbling and mumbling he pushes
the paper away as if used for a smear
on a soiled arse, or an alcoholic's
snotty nose, and smiles at me vaguely.

The smile defeats any moisture
he may have inside his critical
skeleton wrapped in yellowy skin.
Then he walks back to his desk
to wait for the next riddle of
bullet holed written rubbish
from the circus that is my job.

Shards of colour

I paint the world in the wet,
in colours mixed with liquid light,
and like tears of love, reality emerges
and seals itself therein.

The dormant awakes everywhere,
in my silence, in my journey,
and like the joy of happiness,
truth emerges and beauty stands.

An empty space in the universe
offers itself up to the feast before it.
Colours as miracles, drops of God's
love for the immensity before us all.

I wash my hands after the day's work,
the colours trickle from my fingers
like fish with sacred wings, I am given
these tiny shards of shimmering miracles,
and then when I wake the following day,
to my surprise, I find small traces remain
to remind me to rejoice in them again.

Strength

The swan in me senses peace,
gliding easily on the liquid serenity in my life.
Generosity is never far from the open heart.

The bull in me crashes into invisible walls
leaving raw bruises on myself and others.

Mighty wings cradle love and hope
as the horns lock other horns bitterly
in the maelstrom of this, our chaotic life.

The giddy shadows and sunlight
inhabit both, dripping, filling and spilling.

I seek peace and truth, away from false power
into the spaces of the forever, of the better nature.

The swan in me is also the butterfly – delicate and strong –
elegant and fragile – knowing and unknowing – beautiful.

The bull in me is also the hound – fighting and charging –
fierce and furious – savage and brash – fractious.

I subjugate the one and embrace the other
and find inner strength and peace along the way.

Tale of the Sea

When I was young the sea spat salt at my long hair
aiding in its destruction. But at the time powdered me
salty across my skull and body, making my face
sprinkled and lips tasty. I was polluted with its abrasive
deposit. My skin peeled off revealing pinkish flesh,
as the sun left imprints of power and strength over me.
Eventually I became the colour of roasted peanuts.

In the water, the moving sand threatened to cut me up as my body
scrolled and I dived to save my life from the dinosaur-sized waves:
I blindly swivelled and curved in and out of its arrogance fearlessly.

My mother - nervous as a ten-footed crab - sprinted up and down
the beach of many deaths, searching for me, shielding the sun from
her glistening face and made-up eyes, scanning the over-crowded beach
telescopically to ensure I hadn't twisted and tumbled towards the depths
of the sea's unpenetrable domain never to return to the surface again.

After a while I came up, very quietly, behind her, and tapped her
loudly on the shoulder, to receive swiftly - within a split second -
an enormous slap around my grinning face. This came from the depths
of her shock: deeper than my fears or the fears from sailors who
refuse to swim and worry at what they thought lay beneath
the canopy of a nautical mile.

She marched off, treading big trouble, sulking for the rest of
the day and evening.
The anger of her love knew no boundaries and dominated over
me like an ocean.

The Daffs Brightened Up My Billet

The rain has settled.

The sun hits the Gray's Inn Road, the glare begins to dehydrate.

The flowers grow too early: one day too cold - one day too hot.

They have an unsure fate amongst any sensible monkey.

The daffodils will survive the next earth age.

And why not? The flower that welcomes springtime

Reflects the yellow of the sun, does so before it arrives.

Bright exterior, bright interiors,

bland business designs pervade everywhere.

You can only buy so many daffs to the pound.

The favourite flower of aunties who used to be daughters

of bed and breakfast owners in seaside Margate,

saying 'hello ducks', eating little pinkie cakes

and gossiping their friend's flo's fate.

No park keeper should mind the stealing

of a few from each patch of a dozen or so.

My favourite flower with tulips and roses

call love and posies to my heart, and brighten up my loo.

The embroidering of time

I have considered
the greater universe
of what we are together,
the transverse of our weave,
the transfer of one thread
over and above another.
The weft of our story
created from the yarn
of what we have been.

We sing those songs
and merge our melody,
to create other sounds,
plunged out of harmony,
shaded in subtlety,
in the union, cascading history
and I wondered at the enormity
of it within the shared horizon.

We will watch
thread embroider time
about us,
knitting the many lives
in this greater conspiracy,
in the consideration of liberty.

Together in combination,
in the great conversation
of our immense creation,
the beginning of individuality
that will carpet across space
Straddling past us both
to travel to the greater unknown.

This, your story, has begun
my growing, beautiful son.

The end of my cats

My ginger tom breathed leukaemia for a week and died.
I squeezed water through a pipette into him
when all hope was lost.
His face froze when he was injected a huge amount
of clear anaesthetic until his eyes blinked no more.
My tears substituted his, reminding me of how much
I still had to cry for my life,
reminding me that I had been relatively young
when his life had ended, but he was old so that was alright.

The vet was having a normal day,
without incident when this friend I had known for
over 16 years had to die, when we decided - when I said so.

Within a month my other cat - a tortoiseshell - was dead.
His thyroid finally disabled his senses until he scratched
and bumped into the furniture with both his retinas detached,
his hearing gone and his nose redundant.
He was alive but dead to the veterinary profession.
I cried some more, but less. Another witness of me gone.
I thought, no more cats for the moment.

The garden at Buglose, France

The garden yawns itself into daylight time
and the acrobatic bats have hidden deep
within the aged house-beams for rest
and an unswerving peaceful sleep.

Wet from recent rain, droplets
keep gobbing at nature's living blend.
Cockerels begin their throaty yell,
a wheeze and a full intake of air and then
a comical song, broken with a twisted melody.

The garden is silent, elegant and just simple
from here. I am fooled from my vantage
point as I see little of the effort involved.
The garden has fruit and vegetables that
I can pick and eat and are as sweet with
their generosity as is sour the immensity
of man's industry.

Am I naïve in thinking there should be gardens
for everyone to enjoy a little, to plant a little,
to love and cultivate thought?
A garden has no emotion until I think of one.
The cockerel calls all to attention.

The ghost of my grandmother

I feared her when I was told she had died.
Too young to understand my imagination
through spooky stories that scared my sleep.
The hospital smelled of stone and tears, of loss.
You heard echoed voices; wheels screamed
and screeched up and down municipal corridors.
Inescapable scars questioned the lives of adults,
as the past became the total world back home.
Silent memories on mantle pieces, a squashed armchair,
redundant slippers, human dust.
I remember standing on the landing at home being told
of her lost humanity. We were all now spectators
in the numbing ritual of her exit.

I feared her ghost from stupid stories my older brother planted.
I was eleven, twelve years old. I cried and was not talked to;
I irritated and cried some more.
I became a problem and could not be brushed under the carpet.
A couple of weeks later I slept in a boarding school dormitory.
Before that, I slept in her bedroom filled with stuffed animals.
The Alsatian pelt with a fixed growl was as eerie as the tales
of darkness and shadows. I remember a book of ghost stories
illustrated with an owl perched on a gravestone on a moonlit
night that terrified me even if I never read the pages inside.
My grandmother had died and the corruption was final.
I embraced her memory through the filters of my own making.

The search for wings

I suckled her music into me,
a duet with my mother's
swollen breast and hot milk.
She pumped,
flooding my core
as I gasped existence
into the greater fabric of life.

The forced desire to be fed
overwhelmed and I greedily
mouthed her teat
for a bellyful of humanity,
I swallowed my future deeply.

My mother sang
the imperious song
of damned eternity
as she forced herself into me.

I have no memory of her pushing,
when I left the immensity of her womb
and the light pinched my dormant senses.

The gods of breathing nature attacked
as the bacterium of time began to tick,
my fiery wings fell from possibility
and the search for the everlasting
as I landed in the span of my life.

The truth about our family

I will ask for stories of our family from you, my mother.
I will ask you to turn the many pages of your past
from the memory of the idea of what is truth and fiction,
to offer some sense of why there are us and who we were.

There is a photo of a child sitting on the grass
in between his father's legs. His father is smoking.
They both look happy, although sitting on a lawn in Kent
was unusual for the father, without the collapse of alcohol
above and below his ground, he was never rooted.

There are the fantasies of a child, half-baked, raw
and unrealised. There are many holes in the ground,
you can read tombstones that will never answer back.

Half-remembered people you knew, who knew you
who are now gone, days that smelt of memories
in the season's fastening progress,
a muffled sound of lost tears rests in the atmosphere forever.
A trivial consumer thing can become a profound souvenir.

Speaking of names that meant nothing to the child,
exploits retold over again boring the daylight out the young
over a meal on holiday. Everyone had died apparently.
Adults chatted in the sad eyes of sombre rooms,
listing foundations in the echoed history of southern France.

The family switched off, faded feebly, flickering faintly.
The strength and weakness extinguished in the private dust
of crumbling damp buildings, between stained sheets
and mattresses of warfare and bad medicine.
The ancient mathematics of our DNA was just stupid numbers.

Sun Flowing

US

A field of poppies

I want to sleep in the heat of a summer poppy field with you
and drowsily recall those fiery ruby nights we spent together.

I want us to roll recklessly on impractically delicate blooms
that jut their vibrant colour to the solar heat above drowsily.

We could shelter in them, emulating their beauty as we hear the loud
forces on the hurry of others who run by, we would renew ourselves
and like flowers opening, we would be exposed to each other's rays.

We could fall asleep in the spread of a field until the chill of night
awakens us and we leave the carpet of closed flowers to dream
for us as we stretch to the radiant elevating heat between us.

A union made

Warm red curls tickle my chest with smooth slow-motion kissing.
In heat barely felt sprigs of downy tremble-feel, explore my skin
with moist lip, succulence tasted, eyes closed and amplified senses.

The unseen connection tangles our honey embrace of liquid limbs
sculpting, holding bare skinned form until melting harmony sings,
uniting the tempo of exhilaration, affecting the arousal of the inner.

The literal exists, exciting in combination, a duet seen and unseen.
Sensuous fingers give and take as trickles of perspiration squeeze
from open fenestration, an ocean of pores in a lush garden watered.

And fertility inspires and grows. The body grows in its importance
relating to the other in a dialogue erotic, sexual populates, chatters,
uniting creatively, a cadenza unknown, untried in tickles and kisses.

Passive and active, conscious of thought and action surrounds easily
and vanishes completely, our natural body dance is exchanged always,
glistening, leaving the body exhausted in laughter and a union is made.

Always the coolest of doorways

It wasn't necessarily the best of times
or the best of me, the best of wines
or the best of you, the warmest of nights,
the brightest of moons, the nicest of streets,
the trendiest of bars in the smart part of town.

We didn't have the cleverest of talks,
sit at the best of tables, with the cleanest of napkins.
My pockets weren't the fullest, as the moths attested.
I wasn't at my wealthiest, or my smartest,
or wearing the shiniest shoes with the strongest of laces,
chewing with the whitest of teeth in the kindest of moods.
We certainly weren't coy about our agenda that night.

It wasn't as if I didn't know you or I didn't want you,
or I wouldn't try or hadn't had; I wanted what I wanted
and slowly the alcohol took hold and awoke the desiring,
and you could've imagined a better seduction,
as the night could've been the dullest ever
without wanting to or trying the making of love to you.

But wasn't the moon the fullest, and weren't we the closest,
didn't we feel the passion and violence of the kissing, the biting,
struggling in a moment of an explosive erotic experience.
Didn't we search for privacy in the dirty streets that night?
Weren't we two bellyfuls of red wine in the emptying city,
swaggering and swollen, swaying in a London doorway,
hidden from the pace of hectic pedestrians.

Hadn't we become the most romantic of couples
in our boozy, breathy pairing, as we locked tight together
and vanished completely in a haze of shaky memories that night.

As good friends do

We need a place we can meet
and not just the pulsing wires and generators,
 or electricity and beams firing at us.

We should remove our shoes and walk in the wet grass
in our feverish imagination together, but really together,
in simple human contact, in the embrace of a smiling face.

Away from locations that risk destruction of our nature,
our Covid held flags, the blackness that desires our souls
make us fear each other irrationally, in abstract instability.

We need to get closer to each other, to communicate,
in the sinew of anticipation, the normality of enthusiasm.

And when the wet grass is dancing between our toes,
and the sounds of living earth is singing its joy for us,
then we will embrace each other, as good friends do.

The Carousel

Boggy birds and muddy boys

Concerned as she is by this dilapidated pond
she launches herself deep into the muddy soup
wearing Gucci sunglasses
and attacks it with a too-small spade.

A sense of humour is rawly needed as we are
all creaking at the toil of repairing this gooey
thumbprint, this methane filled bog.

She and I ask how can these breezy, bright
septagenarians work like garden Trojans.

She in her Gucci's and I collapse exhausted
while they make all of us a fried breakfast.

Dancing into the cream of the night

You said take me dancing
in the cream of the night

like we did that time
when the music was jasper Spanish.

The seated flamenco women clapped
out the velocity of chattering rhythms

pushing the black and scarlet music
to the edge of our half-conscious world,

exciting the bloody pump with the drum
of temptation that agitated our lustiness.

The partnership of limbs tangled
loquacious, heady, demanding.

We took to the slippery dance floor
where I held the spine of your wet skin

in the stretch of my flexed palm –
you said your heart needed to dance with me

until the silver slit cracked into the shock
of the smoky grey marbled morning.

In charged anarchy, we succumbed
to fog drunkenly and lost ourselves till then.

Delight

I've been delighting in your face
since the Eureka mess of our embrace,
the cork of fizzing kissing taken place,
the sexual notation of blushing staves,
a lust-compass flashing up radar blips.

Sloppy corners, edges in melted clips
of our manic laughter, on risky ships,
in the city's darkness and muddy trips,
naked tangles on private sandy strips,
isolated scrub lands and forest bits,
disused canal tunnel with freezing tits,
stopping the car in shadowy lay-bys,
alleyways, echoing blissed-out cries,
she delighted, ripping open my flies.

And through our lustiness a miracle came,
the pneumatic forces created the near-same,
through the acrobatic propagated struggle
in the hospital you pushed out of the bubble
when we saw you delight in your life force.
Now we are celebrating the main course
of us all together, as a loving source,
of the wonderful blended mix,
of our delight, our scented lives transfixed
we have built the home as well as the bricks.

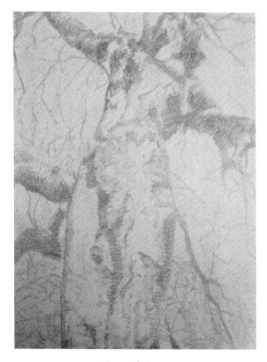

Tree of Hope

Discovering peace at last

The gathering age shelters the trees
That canter around my life, the leaves of which
Blow breezily, allowing light
To flicker between the fronds of thoughts,
Glimpses of questions asked and answered
If the honest eye reaches as far as the dull brain.

A house with a home blends in harmony
At this moment of intensity, of calm.
Serene moments of wakefulness, of levels
Of those I love are separated by their activity.
I ponder them, and myself, a window looking forward,
Inwardly.

To have reached this place in life is a miracle
Of drips and spillages that would never have been imagined.
I sheltered behind my life, looking at the shadows
Dance around me, listening to myself speaking,
Turning my head away from oblique depths and tragedies.

There must have been a moment of directional changes,
Of a road and a road splicing through me, taking me
To a different and unknown place, to allow all your joy
To live in my heart after such battles were lost and won.
Now prayers are answered, hopes fulfilled, peace at last.

Expensive words

She wants the poem to be beautiful,
expansive in the rent of words used,
the sludge of bad language kept away,
for the lexicon to throb in radiant joy.

I know what she wants from words,
a garden of goodness, a sense of the outdoors,
away from the trench of personal darkness,
into the brightness that our own souls capture,
not a strangeness preserved, nor perverse,
a shimmer of cool, not icy, a warmth inviting.

She demands gently, away from rigid reality,
the continuing poverty of hardships are just
put-upon-sensitivity to trap our ignorance.

For us to grow and connect with elegance
may seem trivial in this hammer-hard world,
but the truth is different, it is a servant
to the comfortable and the comforted
that can heal and repeal the sadness within,
and the power of words float gently towards us.

Flowers

She offers me the light of her peace
into this flickering cavern that can be life.
Sometimes there is only air to breathe,
where the filter of hope cracks through,
shifting the powerful rays illuminated
when I am not looking too hard.
She has expressed her planet of love
and the chance of walking deeply
into her mind's grass barefooted.
She loves flowers
and breathes in their scent fully.
I am a flower to her.

Giving in and giving up

I can't fault her logic; with children it is wise to listen to mother.
Our home shudders, wails and tears rip into our brain,
eyes blanche, ears lacerate, we droop, we sag, though we can take it.

We need to reverse the 'made-up' story at a painful 02.30am,
we need to give him everything and nothing,
and put a bleary full-stop to get back to sleep.

I crash about angry, up and down stairs,
she crashes about angry with me,
we skirmish while trying to soothe our wet-faced son.

A story may be the only answer; we may be defeated this time,
'bad' parents always give in to their infants,
'good' parents give to their children without giving in.

I leave my wife to soothe our boy in whatever way she can
and go back to bed, a flicker of sleep returns.

Holding firm and fast

She tumbled towards me, slowing down her time and noticed the movements of a stranger in front of her, his eyes blinking. Her mouth spoke to familiar faces, conversations often had continued until we shared the same space together and talked, our mouths began to move the voices of searching for each other.

The risk stepped forward, the warnings were lightly trodden, warily and carefully walking each worried moment sparingly.

And then, night time collided with the stark light of daytime reality, of shaking the branches vigorously, of fruit falling, nectar supped.

Spellbinding dances in darkened places; kisses unwarranted or demanded, sombre alleyways of sodden drunken displacements left a racing peril of possibilities.

I watched the heart rise in your eyes, your pout dilating red fleshed lips for the kiss, the hip cloistered magnetically, demanding, pushing forward.

We wanted to be on the street of noise and bluster, and family warned you against our thunder, our coupled fury, of my shadows.

Then, I married you and we formed battlements that still hold firm and fast.

More time with each other

We rise when the yellow and blue begins,
coffee fuels and we rapid-drive to the sand,
on the way we listen to inferior sons
of the Velvet Underground.

Our skin pales less than time that passes just before
in the pollution-balloon of the city we are stuck in.

The Frisbee becomes a glossed out surreal magazine UFO,
shaped as it eclipses the forces above and air dances for us.

Walking on the water with arms up catapults away
the seat that postures us from the scarring of our slave lives,
and it takes the blood off the walls,
and removes the beast from our intolerance.

The liquid ellipse horizons before the two of us,
names become pointless instantly,
we gain sex appeal and the spears
we held and caves we lived in,
distortions maybe,
but the colour needles out thin time
and leaves us with more of each other.

On the Banks of the Old Canal

We have known how to have good times you and I.
The absurdities of our objectives, unrefined
and sometimes unwitting, makes us smile
in that secretive way that only old friends
know how to involving no red faces or shame.

Our first phase involved some pain and confusion,
but this one is more like fun do you not agree?

We scour the banks of the canal
for broken pieces of ceramics
to decorate your garden paradise.
I find old, empty bottles for me
to collect and save. More things
for my impoverished idea of antiques.
Our second phase is pleasing and easy.

Less baggage filled, less objectives
and scenarios compete, as you run towards another
youthful lover, incorrigible and free.

Our beautiful garden

My son, I hear you play
your sound machine,
pressing keys
of miracles and beauty.
The voice is developing
brilliantly, like pebbles
flickering in reflective
colours, I listen to sparkles
shimmering.

Your father's so proud,
and his heart grows in endearment.

What is love? So often asked:
a powerful feeling of intent
and pursuit, chased by the exhausted,
the anxious, the promise fulfilled?
Singers sing, writers write.
The hope of lover's weep for love to love.

I listen and wait here alone,
and then when you come home,
I listen with you too.
Our garden grows in sound and time.
Such a beautiful bloom opening its petals.

Softness

Winter greens darken and the sky
becomes dense grey through the window
of a family home.

I stroke your face softer as the colours
of your hair retain the softness
of other colours, the hue of life.

I stroke your face through your hair
and back again, the softness of love.

The new house smells of wood and children,
the chaos of things alive.

The piano music of Couperin
is organised chaos and soft and hard edges.

It all fits well here.

Something ancient and something
of the very now is emerging.

Colours continue to darken outside,
the mix of voices and footsteps,
activity in the unsubstantial, the trivial
is important, almost mystical and fleeting.

One can hear the whisper of God in it.

Sunday roast with my friends Grappa & Calvados

Calvados and Grappa drunk after a lamb lunch,
with red wine and redder faces during the meal,
a two-day hangover leaves me wasted for more.

Thirty years since winning an Observer poetry prize
mentioned as if the day after yesterday just happened.
Time cancelled time out, as we sipped at human memory
and the echoed gong of written-out-loud words rewarded.
The airless moment of silences fills with wishes and misery,
sliding down the slosh of a high-octane fuelled Sunday roast.

These are the titles I wrote, this is my favourite,
and she likes it too, pointing to his smiling wife
cupping her eyes in her head with both hands.

We smoke Cuban cigars and gain sophistication,
blowing rings around our drowsy pontification.
I read elegant lines, tuneful, desired. The short-form
envelopes this Huguenot house with brisk musicality.

We compete for air; we pluck laurels to show them off.
One poem in an anthology of a hundred and fifty is short fry,
but I still smile the sadness of a little less failure than yesterday.

The art of divisibility

She wants my time
but not in rows of measures
or in the control of mathematics
but in the hidden measurements
of being together, of feeling
without addition or subtraction.

Having someone's space in time
is all that can be truly given freely.
When we adjust so time does,
as we shift to the warmth of company,

which is what can be said
for these moments of value
to be understood as precious.

We control time and divide it into two,
an equal share for both of us, as we
become living geometry and curve
around each other's cogent and form.

The battlefield is drawn

Our artillery is mostly muffled
as we take aim in gentle ways,
the shells are filled with wit
sprinkled with sarcasm for fun.
We practice low-level conflict
and fire incendiaries at each other
that we easily dust ourselves off from.

Our warfare is an arena
of foolishness and stupidity,
we try to gain ground from
inert cannons and friendly fire.
We charge like fickle soldiers
who really don't want a fight,
we say make love not war.

We find an armistice is agreed on
as I cook and you do the washing up.

The French motorway

The road is a long gape; teeth gnaw into the rubber tires.
I drive too fast for it to bite well; the wheels attack the road,
my eyes close without knowledge, a trap hidden in the brain.
Encased we sleep, muffled within a box, my son in his seat,
my wife beside me and myself, all unconscious, unconcerned.

Suddenly a jolt attacks, the bite snaps, the car flies uncontrollably.
My wife jolts, grabs the wheel. I wake befuddled and push her away.
I snatch the wheel off her as we hurtle, both screaming confusedly.
The car takes off; my son remains silent behind us both.
The tarmac slips, we dive into grass and yellow flowers.
Teeth no longer grip, the wheels melt, and we are awake but asleep,
I try to control the car, and it bumps and slides in and out of my fingers.

My thumb bleeds deeply from a day old wound. We halt violently.
The motorway roars, I steer the carcass out of danger.
We say to each other, 'are you alright?'
Flowers and mud stick in the radiator, smiling green from
the confusion.
A near miss leaves the breath of a nightmare behind us
and the future trauma pollutes my sleep just before
I crash into my pillow.

The new notebook

A new page whispers for a voice,
a new notebook on my ready lips
saying seduce me now,
take my virgin plains and describe
your point, take the pen and water
your virtues, shimmer the language
approved in nature, put voice to ink,
to the groove that indents
and let your voice flow all over me.

Take dreams and imagination,
to the place of sunsets and sunrises,
do not waste my inner beauty,
give it to yourself now and write.

THEM

A black woman and a white man

A black woman and a white man

She yelped for her husband at the crematorium

holding onto his nephew, a small woman gripping,

covered by a large man's body.

Her hand pulling at his coat.

A black woman and a white man, an arm and a hand,

tearing at cloth. She called for a miracle.

The coffin, slowly, ever so dignified, disappeared downwards.

Afterwards we went to the church hall and she served me

warm soup in a plastic cup on a frozen day.

A love song in the time of pestilence

I shall not ask for your hand in marriage without a mask on your face.
Surprises are like viruses that diminish the potencies of passions.
Do not touch my body when you brush past me on a cool summer
evening of shaded trees and spotlighted cars rushing by who knows where.
Gather your feelings when your bloom flowers, when your jogging body
passes mine so close. I can smell your breakfast to come, your feuds
with your flatmates, the flimsy secrets you keep hidden in your devices.
I will not kiss that mouth so riddled with words of apology until proof
of freedom from the rotten pestilence has been known to be crushed,
or not at all within the breath of your salty mouth and carefree attitudes
towards the sex you never have that emanates purely from flippancy.
Carry no bags for me when trying to be kind, do not iron my clothes, pass
my toothbrush, gargle words of disinfection or amnesties.
You want to love me? Well keep two meters away and take your clothes off
so I can gaze upon your body safely while exploring my own fervent feelings.
I do love your dance of possible death, the grace of the zips and buttons
undone for me in these thrilling times. And afterwards, well after all this
cantering and touching imagination, I may reach out and you can rest your
fruit on my finger when you are completely clean of the disasters of viruses.

A violin called 'Hope'

The pause in movement, the cut and carve sanded.

From the beginning

there stands a man poised in a miracle
within small spaces of time, in a deep tempo,
the craftsman takes wood from nature for in his vision stems
a sound and gives birth slowly to the instrument within his sight.

The love child is curved and vaulted, in the air of magical wealth,
bestriding the very nature of time, he gives birth to the beginning
of sound.

Braille

The smooth space, twice my hand-span
stretches across and tingles below the mound,
electrifying my thoughts into an immense generator.
I slide my touch to the surface as it warms to my desire,
small bumps protrude rhythmically from it into an order
as a silent voice slowly, melodiously becomes disarmed
and begins to amplify in me and communicate to me,
and begins at the beginning of a story to be told, a story.
That voice starts to laugh, or to be scared, actually talks
describing all types of seen objects and narratives
as well as the secrets unseen that I know so well inside.
There are also those murderous exploits of jealous eyes
or the floating love of contact through the mind's eye
that jumps out at me with the character's shocked out lives.
Things that I know immediately also have meaning
From this sloping, smooth bumpy surface that starts and stops
with the speed from my fingers and palm and it is my place
that is kept that way just as long as I need it to be, just for me.
I have been exploring this immense freedom since childhood
and it has expanded me and given to me to take as I climb
the storytelling mountain of words to eventually float in them.

Chickens and dead horses

He spoke of villages, of this time and before.
Kentish homesteads scented along ancient mulch-tracks,
scoring the scarred chalk, closing in towards the sea.

Life never-ending, life and death danced
in cool grey-stone churches and shabby drinking houses.

Villages, some from Doomsday and invisible
in earth-green landscape shared a continuum of sorts.

And those trees, you know in slack rows were planted
with dead horses buried below them. Old avenues
stand to strident attention, death in life bled essence,
slow released chemicals and stuff oozed to the root.
Their last gallop strengthened and pushed towards heaven.

And then he said chickens in China
chucked in holes by cultivators quaked alive.
Someone said to him why bother killing them
as they will die anyway, as muffled sounds of life-forces are
slowly suffocated,
dirt overtakes and snuffs them out.

Climate Change Talks

Bombs are puffs of smoke
in comparison to these efforts.
People are messy animals
who fret and frown, about this and that,
around big tables in important places,
as black meets white
and languages are garbled
with respectable regularity.

Cannons and car bombs
will be wisps of air if you look at the gasps
from the poor gathering crops with empty lungs
in acrid forests of empty spaces
and carcasses of hope,
dead around poisoned prisons
where Eden once breathed.

Lights will deafen as night will have no repose
to the burning winds and sooty seas,
and the walls we build will protect only sandstorms
as reality sears through life
like burning butterfly wings under magnifying glasses.

Puffs of smoke, wisps of air, the stampede of time,
the fear from false gods, of men and machines
with the logic of power; the fear of the wealthy
smiling benignly. The scorching sun will be
a lynch-mob with no jury and hope of clemency.

She

The fruit touches her lips of pomegranate and dew-moist
juice trickles onto her and settles puddle shaped.
She is energised, excited by her need for sexual contact.
She becomes orgasm and metaphor, a smell of life invades
as she eats her baby's placenta: he is magic, safe in her arms.
She lies on her bed of leaves and fur next to the new-born.
The bed smells of musk and shadows.
Night simmers, the baby sleeps and the mother hunts meat.
A bird screeches and dives blindly towards a sharp-ended spear.
Blood thrills and an umbrella of feathers will become the cave,
bones will decorate and sharpened needles, the head and legs,
a fetish to prevent spirits stealing her babe like the last two.
The sticky warm fluid dyes her hands and she is primal,
waiting for him to take her to the waters where she can swim
and hunt amongst the precious stones and tickle-fish.
When tree and stone weep it is for the world she knows,
the world that slowly disappears into unknown pools,
mysteries of nowhere, where the food is when she asks for it.
Beasts make sounds of night-colours to steer her to safety.
She hugs herself and masturbates till she sleeps and dreams
his return, when she will spread her church body hollow into
his for the next harvest to be reaped. She sleeps.

The kiss of death flogged my life away

He held my soul and cradled my anticipation,
he entered my thoughts and kissed away my life.

The seduction stealthily slinked and whispered,
those robbed kisses, he was too strong for me.

His love loved me as we met in secrecy,
I did not want to be trapped without his embrace.

He carried his heart and took me to my punishment,
to my scars, to the wrath of his compassionate eyes.

And then, there, my family watched me being flogged
for my correction, for the pride of a husband I did not love.

My flesh became ecstatic and flowed like a mystic river,
my back bled for the angry eyes, to the injustice of life.

My body was destroyed, skin flayed away, and I have paid
with a broken mind ever since, drowning in the agony of that day.

Soon I will be taken to a hot place and be buried to my mouth
of many tendernesses in a standing position, and then my judges

Will surround me with justice, with an ancient law and look
me proud in the face and stone my poor head and face to death.

Afterwards they will walk away with theirs fixed in righteousness.

The Lament of the HS2 Tree

I heard pipes and drums, of men crossing fields
treading on the mist of a morning when I was sapling.
The battle took place around my soil,
where my lifespan started, men dripped blood on me.
Their hot varnish splattered scarlet onto my young leaves.

The times, they buried men and women, drummers and fifers fell,
Children left their earthly life before they could breathe regret for it.
Amorous lovers kissed under my powerful trunk in hope for future times.

I grew and swelled, looking at my sky blue and wet, of heat and cold
mingling in a communion of circular harmony above and below me.
I loved and celebrated the community that lived around and
amongst me.

We skipped to the chaos of scrabbling squirrels, to those naughty
robins, pilfering erratically, to the ants scurrying purposely,
in patterns of movement. In me was Eden, protected and valuable
in a constant dialogue naturally.

And then, I remembered the crash of industry and the grinning smell
of oil and steams burning the sky with mouthfuls bellowing smoke.
My companions felt unwell, as metal boxes sped past us all.
We bore the poison and noise. My Eden of friends hid inside me.
The stink of molten tar pressed close to our nature and suffocated.

And now I am asunder, defeated and broken. My fibres are torn,
My roots bleed and scream lament. All around is confusion and
fruitlessness.

I am mourned by the flying ones, ants, squirrels, they are poor
children, confused.

We will never again rustle leaf, play on my branches,
look on the panoramic beauty above the canopy of living carpet.
The coming train line has killed me as I slowly return to dust.

The Lioness

She roars the day as a she-lion
covered in the sun's spillage,
and in her beauty and savagery
covets closely her children,
protecting them,
deterring the dangerous world
around her and them away.

And as she purrs in her golden aura
I imagine with blind eyes her gaze.

The glow of her form intensifies
in a graceful ballet of life movements.

She explains herself easily
and cranes her thoughts in amber tears,
in the shades at the wonder of words
and the unremitting world around her.

The Norwegian mother

She walks thinly along the narrow road
back to the school, as I walk towards her.
We stop and talk. She tells me that her
Illness has spread to her head. Her hand
radars around her face grimly.
What can you do? You carry on as you do
when you have three young children
who need your care. My family in Norway
are no help, nor is my husband's here.
He has given up work to care for the kids.
Who cares for you? I ask.
Have you a good community around you?
The women of the mosque come round
with food every day.
They feed my husband and the family.
You carry on and don't think about the future.
She looks at her watch. I apologise for taking up
her time. There is a recorder concert, she grins,
and presses ears in pretence of pain as she walks on.

The raft of the refugees

We do not look at their exhausted faces,
Into the experience of their shattered eyes. We ignore, we hide.

The waters are knives cutting deeply into flesh, swallowing
The wailing choir of death of salt tears sobbing for liberty and life.

There was hope of peace and safety after the insane panic,
Of running away, of other shores were made. Bundling old and young.

Then being robbed of all options and crowded into space,
Setting sail, squinting and blinking towards dangerous currents.

You may ask where is home for your children, where is a place
for your old?
Where are your scars of insane doctrines, where does hope lie
for your others?

Here, how we lumber, fat and frigid.
Talking big on little islands of our judgemental minds,
of our hateful words for the other.

No empathy exists in the straits of the humanity bubble,
gurgling its last breath,
Crying out for a home in a place of only hatred and more poverty
and violence.

Bodies bloat and rot, floating flotsam and jetsam of our world
vanish in the sharp waters.

The Secret language of words

From this empty page
we invade the stillness
and open pastureland...

I, the letter, and I the next –
we are harvested, gathered for the task,
shuffled and organised.
With the multitude & (of) our brethren,
(and) together we rule.

The scope goes beyond the literate,
(or the illiterate)
the secret language of letters
is a world within a world
(which can be added or removed).

(this/which only works for man
when he tames and herds
and learns to understand
so little from vastness).

Verbs are our gazelles
conjunctions, our flora,
exclamation marks, our comedians,
adjectives our artistic nature!
Keyboard letters are our bombardiers.
Fire! Rapid fire!!

Our paradise dominates all we survey
on man's surface living life of alliteration.

And with a P.T.O we dominate again

I, our god.

I say, I say, I say, entertains us when comedians are asleep.

We, our mother. Us, we are us together.

We know all the secrets that are missed and misspelled –
all infinite detail was given to us aeons ago –
before the birth of pictograms.

Articles police us and scare children with
stories of rubbers, deletions and extinction.
We are the beauty standing on the foundation of man's very existence.
Without us, total collapse of the very nature of rarefied man would
cease to exist in any great importance. You would babble and bawl,
struggle and fall. Call your mothers, call your gods, and bark like dogs,
croak like frogs. The beauty of our history would be lost forever and so
would man's progression and dreary institutions.

Capitals facilitate minuscules that facilitate majuscules, which
facilitate capitals.

Apostrophes skip and dance for us.
Our priests are semicolons, our nun's colons.
Together they supervise our clear path across
the sentence, looking after big pushes for building
The bricks of our paragraphs: books our towns,
libraries, empires and cities...

We can leave great gaping holes if we wish to!

Please turn the page is another ploy for our hunger and
irrepressible path.

Follow the arrow ➜

Poetry teaches us love.
Dot, dot, dot disciplines dimwits.

Can you hear the laugher of my brothers and sisters?
As they conjunct and form phrases of infinite
pleasure and happiness.

If you try to scratch the surface, we block you by inventing
Another language for you to puzzle over. Invent and divide.

000 numbers are our foot soldiers that never deplete.

I, the letter, with I, another letter, and I, yet another letter
(I, also with brothers and sisters & a few more join us for a party)

With this, We say, 'The End'!

The Sound of Blossom falling

He talks of her with the simple love of a father,
describing how they walked the verdant path
and along the softness of the hardy hills
entwined in each other's presence.

He feeds the dialogue of his love of nature
as he gazes and points out
the crisp colours and myriad greens –

he asks if she sees what he sees,
if she hears what he hears –

and as she looks and thinks
with a bright child's mind
she says 'I can hear the sound of blossom falling.'

They both stand still and listen for a moment.

Who told who what

Theo told Guy and Guy told Declan
and Declan told Anne who told me
you were dead.
I told your ex-Chloe
and Chloe told your mother.
Jamie, your brother was told by Anne.
Philippa, your social worker already
knew for two days but told no one,
we had to find out from each other.
Jamie spoke to your mother
and your brothers and sister.
I told other friends who told me
they would come to your funeral.
The Crisis centre said they couldn't talk to me
due to the Data Protection Act.
I couldn't confirm any of the stories I was told.
The centre said they would get in touch
with me after checking who I was, but didn't.
I was still waiting when I knew you had died.

Working in ITU Dept at a time of Covid 19

You cried for those eyes that felt no warmth,
for the afterthoughts of conversations yet to be finished.
The utter confinement gave little comfort in the dying cold
of pipes and masks, the smacking of latex gloves
trapping hands in sweaty health, the fear of a closing down.

The complete violation of sleep's healing process,
static and dispassionate, mechanical air forced through.
The healthy milling around big bodies on small beds,
in plastic bubbles, lying on their bellies with loved ones far away.

Vincent Berquez bio

Vincent Berquez is a poet and artist, living in London with his wife and son. He was born to French parents and attended the French Lycée and Cannock boarding school. He studied Fine Art at Goldsmith's; followed by The Camden Institute, where he was taught by Frank Auerbach. He worked as an artist for many years prior to studying museology and conservation at London University following which he worked as a curator and conserver at various institutions, including the British Museum, and the Louvre.

He has exhibited art in London, Chicago, Germany, Japan, and Italy. His work has appeared in the collection of Charles Saatchi, as well as being featured with the group, Fleurs du Mal. He is represented by the Langham Gallery in London.

His love of poetry began at boarding school, being inspired by his English teacher on the value of the poetic form; and his tone is lyrical and musical. He has been published widely and has recited his work, as well as being in poetry groups, most of his adult life.

He was invited to write a Tribute as part of the 'Poems to the American People' for the Hastings International Poetry Festival for 9/11; and was commissioned to write a eulogy by the son of Chief Albert Nwanzi Okoluko, the Ogimma Obi of Ogwashi-Uku to commemorate the death of his father in Nigeria. He was included in the collection, 'In Protest', 150 Poems about Human Rights with the Institute of English Studies at the University of London; he contributed poems to the edition of 'A Generation Defining Itself'; and has been published in many collections and anthologies, including Decanto, Reflections, and London Voices.

He has collaborated with Scottish composer, Clive Strutt, and a US film maker to produce a song-cycle of seven of his poems for mezzo-soprano and solo piano. These were recorded at the Royal College of Music under the directorship of the concert pianist, Julian Jacobson. He made a poetry film that was shown at a Polish/British festival in London. He also published a private collection of poetry, called, 'Holy Mountain', about the lives of the Orthodox monks on Mount Athos. v.berquez@talk21.com

Printed in Great Britain
by Amazon